I0448940

Letters To My Teen-age Daughter(s)

Letters To My Teen-age Daughter(s)

Terry Camper

To order additional copies of this book, contact:
Xlibris Corporation
1-888-795-4274
www.Xlibris.com
Orders@Xlibris.com
88947

Contents

This book is dedicated to my darling daughter, Tee Cee and to every other teenage female that yearns for, but does not have a father figure to offer her advice on the trials and tribulations she faces as a young lady.

Stay strong! Stay focussed!
Above all, "Keep yo' head up!"

Preface

This, **Letters To My Daughter(s)**, being my initial endeavor into the literary world has been a project a long time in the making. To be exact, it has been fourteen years in the making.

When my daughter, Tee Cee, was nine days old, my wife got a call from the Arkansas Department of Human Services informing us that the child we had registered to adopt was finally ready to be placed in our home. Immediately after getting off the phone with our caseworker, Rosemary McIntosh, Lisa gave me the call that would forever change our lives in ways we could not begin to imagine. To this day, I can honestly say each and every one of the changes has definitely been positive.

When she placed her call to me, I was working as a deputy with the Pulaski County Sheriff's Office. Days earlier, I informed my superiors that I was expecting the call from DHS. Upon receiving the call, I phoned Cpl. Austin. I still remember what he told me. "Go get your baby, Camper!"

After picking up Lisa from the house, we took the five minute drive to Doctor's Hospital. When we entered the nursery there were at least seven infants. Six of them were crying. There was one child that had been placed in the midst of the others. She was the only one not crying. I noticed from the moment I stepped into the room, her eyes had been locked on me. Releasing my wife's hand and heading in the quiet child's direction, I told my wife "This has to be her." After I picked her up, the nurse confirmed that it indeed was her. That began a relationship I never thought I would be in and one that I never knew could change me like it has.

My wife adopted a child and gave birth to another in her first marriage. Of course, when we were united I became Daddy. Back then, I naively thought that that was the most important role I would ever have by far. Those two children were boys and having been raised in a family with both parents raising four boys, I was totally convinced that it was imperative for a boy to have a strong male figure in his life to become a successful person. I was then and still am a proponent of the philosophy "It takes a man to teach a man how to be a man."

After having been in my daughter's life since she was nine days old and having had the experiences we have had, I have broadened my philosophical views. Along with the "Man to be a man" viewpoint, I now realize "It takes the love of a man to raise a girl into a lady."

I started writing letters to Tee Cee when she became involved in extracurricular activities that cut into the father/daughter time she and I valued so much. The first one brightened her up so much, I knew then I would have to continue to write them. Also, the joy I received in seeing her face light up made it very easy for me to write them.

When I realized some of the letters I composed would be useful in the education of other young ladies I started putting them into book form.

Some of the letters have sections entitled: *See what you did, here we go again!* This is what my wife, Lisa, tells our children Jonathon, Reggie and Tee Cee when they say something that encourages me to tell one of my many stories of growing up in Brinkley (Bucktown), Arkansas.

In regards to the simplicity of the title, it clearly describes what you are to expect to see when you peruse through the pages for the first time. You will see letters written to "my" daughter(s). Do I have more than one daughter? I have one that resides with my wife and me. Throughout "my" community, I have thousands. Throughout "our" community, I have millions. Just as throughout "your" community, you have thousands. And throughout "our" community, you have millions. We have all heard it before and I am a staunch advocate of the saying "It takes a village to raise a child." I also believe that as our community moves away from supporting this, it allows more decaying in the structural fiber that supports it.

If you are one of those people that are going to ask the question, "Is he vain enough to think he can have an affect on every young lady in our community," here is my answer. Yes! Alone, I know it is impossible for me to physically touch each and every one. Through this book, though, I truly believe I can offer life lessons to every young lady that has the opportunity to read it. And I do believe they "all" should read it.

Terry Camper
Author

Puttin' You Up On Game

Proverbs 31:10—The virtuous woman
"When a woman displays strength of character,
men will notice and treat her accordingly."

Cube,

Let's talk about what can turn out to be the biggest distraction in your life (if you allow it to be.) "The opposite sex." Since you are a girl, of course, let's talk about boys. It may be hard for you to really get a grasp of this thought; but, I, your daddy, used to be a boy just like those you are growing up and going to class with everyday. I entertained the same thoughts and had the same dreams as most of them that make it known to you that they are interested in you. I say most of them because this is a new day and some of the things young men do, the way they conduct themselves around girls (and grown-ups for that matter) and some of the things they say to girls just weren't done back in the day. Did Daddy used to talk with his friends about which girl was the prettiest? Yes! Did Daddy used to talk with his friends about which girl had the best body? Yes! Did Daddy run that immature game on girls trying to get a kiss? Yes! What Daddy didn't do was talk nasty to girls. It was more about respect then. I, as a young man with both parents in the home, was raised to respect my parents, other adults, other guys and more importantly for this letter, young ladies. Word had better not get back to Sueney about one of her boys disrespecting a young lady. And, Lord, have mercy on your soul if it got to back to Walter.

Being a young lady, when it comes to the opposite sex, the most vital word to remember is, as the queen of soul, Aretha Franklin put it, R-E-S-P-E-C-T. You must have respect for the young men that are attracted to you, for those that you are attracted to and for those that you share a mutual attraction. Those young men must also have respect for you and for themselves. A far greater respect is the respect you must have for yourself. You must always carry yourself as an intelligent young lady. This refers to the way you dress, the way you talk and the way you walk. (yes, even down to the grades you make)

There will always be attraction between the sexes. As you know, all of that came about in the Garden of Eden. Every individual aspect of your womanly being will either attract or repel some man somewhere. Something as simple as the shape of your ears will get the attention of some men. Likewise, something as complex as the color of your skin will appeal to some men. When I mention the color of your skin, I don't necessarily mean it will make you alluring to men of other races and nationalities.

Granted, that will be the case sometimes too. Moreso, I am talking about African-American men.

Somewhere down the road, you will run across a man with that 1800's Virginia plantation mentality. This type of "colored" man is only attracted to light skinned women. He has to have him a red-bone. "If she ain't light—bright—and damn near white, she ain't right" for him. Now, let me use a little logic to explain this mulatto loving man. Before western Africa, the mother country we speak of, was invaded and stripped of it's most plentiful resource—its people—most blacks possessed a darker skin color. Not to say they all were exactly the same, just closer to a darker hue. Due to the inception of slavery and the slave-master's lust for the dark skin "wenches" he owned, lighter skinned coloreds were being seen in the U.S. for the first time. These children, having the master's DNA, were obviously treated better than those children that had been conceived by and raised by a slave father and mother. Over the course of time, most of the slaves, having by now lost their identity and any sense of self-confidence, started to reason that since their lighter skinned brothers, sisters and cousins were being treated more favorably, they must simply be better people. Of course, this in turn led some to view them as more attractive. I guess you would also have to factor in the fact that the plantation whites of that time had engrained in most slaves that they were pre-destined by God to be an inferior people.

Let's not even get on how some black men see white women. I will never forget a conversation I had with one of my college buddies. He was telling me about this white girl he met. When I asked if she was good looking, his reply was "She white ain't she!" God is my witness, he is married to a white woman today. They have three beautiful children. Don't get it distorted, though. I also have three beautiful children with skin colors ranging from Hispanic-tan to black man brown to your beautiful milk chocolate.

You've seen the way a lady that walks the street, a prostitute, dresses. Those ladies dress like that to attract a certain type of man. The bottom line is this, if you want to be treated like a queen, you must conduct yourself like a queen. If you conduct yourself as someone that doesn't care how she is treated, young men won't care how they treat you. If you allow young men to talk to and disrespect you any kind of way (verbally, physically and emotionally), they will do it. Always remember this: A woman DEmands respect. A lady COMmands respect. The difference: To demand something, you are adamantly insisting that someone give you what you are desiring at that moment in time. A demand derives from more of a verbal nature. To command is to show that you have absolute authority of the situation. A real lady can walk into a room and without saying a word, have the utmost respect of every man in the room. Now don't get respect and attention confused. (to put it in your generation's vernacular, "Don't get it *twisted*.") If a naked woman walks into a room full of men, she will have the attention of everyone in the room. Will she have their respect? No! I sincerely doubt it. More than likely, they will be wandering if she has some sort of mental or emotional condition. Getting back to the word command, consider our nation's president, Barack Obama. He is the Commander-In-Chief of the armed forces. When he walks onto a military site, everybody knows it. He can walk from the front to the back of the site without saying a word and will have the respect of everybody on base.

In my opinion, Smokey Robinson is the greatest songwriter of all time. He wrote a very popular song entitled "Shop Around." A verse of it says, "Just because you've become a young man, now, there are some things that you don't understand, now. Before you ask some woman for her hand, now—keep your freedom for as long as you can, now. My mama told me—you better shop around." Another song that is very appropriate for this conversation is Lyfe Jennings' "Statistics." The part that is so fitting for this letter is where he gives a list of the things a lady shouldn't do: 1) Don't be a booty call—for young ladies your age, this should be a no-brainer. Simply put, you are too young to be considering sex. 2) If he's in a relationship, leave him alone. If he will cheat on her, he will cheat on you. That goes back to earlier when I suggested that you lay back in the cut and check him out before letting him know your interests. 3) Tell him that you're celibate. The song goes on to say "Tell him if he wants some of your goodies, he's gonna have to work for it." I say, "If he wants some of your goodies, he'll have to work and **'wait'** for it. Teens should not be engaged in sex, especially at your age. 4) Be the person you want to find. Don't be a nickel out here looking for a dime. If you are expecting to hook a good catch, you can't be half-stepping. You have to be what a man considers a good catch.

Let's play a word game. When I say man, what comes to mind? More than likely, you thought woman. They go together. When I say lady, what comes to mind? Gentleman? They go together also. To attract a gentleman, you must conduct yourself as a lady.

Right now, this is not Smokey or Lyfe, this is Daddy telling his daughter to just take your time and not get all caught up in the first young man that tells you that you are beautiful. Not that you aren't beautiful. I tell you that all the time because you really are a lovely young lady. Also, don't get overly absorbed in the first young man that you think is cute. If you want to be real about it, when you see someone that interests you, don't let him know right off the bat. Why? The reason is because some males will take advantage of the fact that you are interested even if he isn't interested in you. Again, just lay back in the cut and observe him for a while. Notice how he behaves around other people. Notice how he behaves in an academic setting. Also, just as if not more important, notice how he behaves around other girls.

Be warned that some young men will tell you literally anything to get your interest. When I say anything, I mean "ANYTHING." The biggest game to avoid is when they play the sympathy card. "My parents (or whoever) just don't understand me. I really do have a good heart. People just take everything I do the wrong way." In the words of the illustrious Ocho Cinco, "Child Please!" If everyone takes everything you do the wrong way, maybe you are doing something wrong. Remember: if everyone is saying you are doing something the wrong way, maybe it's because you are. Sometimes we can go against the grain and reveal a new method of how to do certain things. Don't, however, go against the grain when dealing with young men. If he is accused by everyone of not being able to "Do The Right Thing," I would suggest he work on getting himself right before he looks to get into a relationship. The best thing you can do for yourself when approached by this self-pity promoter is to tell him to take that played out Will Smith—Fresh Prince line to the next girl. That is a definite red flag. If you are trying to keep your life on track and get to your desired point, the last thing you need is some knucklehead throwing himself a pity party at your expense.

On TV, you see story-lines of the good girls always falling for the bad boys. Truth be told, this doesn't happen as often as the producers of prime time television would have you believe. Do some girls attract those type of boys? Of course they do. What these shows don't present to us is what every responsible father of a daughter that has ever walked the earth wants to believe. "WE" believe, with it having been proven time after time, that by giving you a proper male role model, you will grow up knowing the characteristics of a *real* man. You will desire, aspire and require those attributes when you are approached by or approach a suitor. You will know the man in your life will have to possess high morals and standards. You will know the man you are involved with must be working. It can be a job in the early adult stages of his life. Somewhere along the way, he needs to parlay that job into a career. You will know he must be legal. A dope man will not make the cut.

Drug dealers, sad to say, always have and always will have a place in our society. Albeit, this is not a respectable place in the functional portion of our society, they have a spot. Even those that hold positions of high esteem, i.e.—government officials, CEO's of major corporations, doctors, lawyers and so on, don't wish to see their children follow in their footsteps on the illegal side of the law. Later on after that child has reached the late teen-age or early adult age, that parent, who obviously has a warped sense of entitlement and has failed the aforementioned child in the rearing department, just may expect and even encourage the child to board that already in flight one-winged airplane. What is the undeniable fate of an airplane that loses one wing? Ultimately, it will come crashing down.

See what you did? Here we go, again: When my cousin Wayne and I were attending Philander Smith College, there were two girl friends that drew our interest. Of course, we pursued them and let it be known that we were very interested. Being raised like we were, we did it with class. Unbeknownst to us, these young ladies were dating the campus dope men. These brothers were rolling fancy cars and had all the designer labels. I know you say "Whoo, big deal!" Actually, back then it was a big deal.

Today, you see high school kids driving a Mercedes Benz or a BMW. Simply put, it was a serious anomaly back then. You can say our people didn't have the money for extravagant expenses like that back then. I like to think we just had our priorities more in order. To make a long story short: The bad boys got the girls. After spending several tumultuous years of in and out relations, one of the young ladies ended up with two children and no father for them. (Ironically, she literally became a "Good girl gone bad.") This particular young man was killed in a bad drug deal. The other young lady ended up in prison. She got caught up with him in a drug raid. Although I would say she didn't have the personality to sell drugs, you better recognize "Five-O" does believe in guilt by association. Having been a Sheriff's deputy, I have seen so many young ladies come into the system because they were "so in love" with a bad boy.

At this point, I'm not even saying that you will make the right choice when it comes to your first boyfriend. (or all of the ones to follow) What I am saying is, "that if you take your time and get to know the young man you are interested in before allowing your emotions to rush you into something you may truly live to regret, you are more susceptible to making a more fitting choice. Then, the relationship you two seek will have time to strengthen and blossom into a real relationship and not one that is based on sex. If he is really that interested in you, he will wait. Of course, I would prefer that you and he wait until you are married and you both have accomplished your educational goal thus setting you up for your careers. I know a lot of people will say this is an unrealistic goal. The fact that it has happened several times before, lets us know it is possible and you can do it. You know and I know that our community doesn't need another teen-age mom on welfare with a "baby daddy" that doesn't want anything to do with her or the child.

I love you,
Daddy

Never 'Dat

Proverbs 14:1
"A wise woman builds her house (reputation), but
with her hands (mouth & body) the foolish one
tears hers down."

Sugar-cube,

As you know, I am and have been one of the biggest
fans of hip-hop music since its early conception. Back
in the day, the politically correct term was "Rap" music.
What does this type of music, no matter what you call it,
have to do with the topic of this letter? Well, back in the
day when the rap community talked about females, you
may have had some that bordered on being disrespectful;
but, for the most part, it was all about getting with a
girl. They had ways of saying things without just coming
out and blatantly saying them. Now, when you listen to
today's hip-hop artists talk about women, more often
than not, they are incredibly straightforward in telling
you what they want to do with them. More often than
not, the female topics of the songs are referred to in a

very dishonorable manner. I would dare to say, with them making those references, they aren't talking about every female they come in contact with. I don't think you will find many, if any, of those artists refer to their own mothers or daughters as a "bitch" or a "ho." I know! Listen to Eminem talk about his mother. That situation is very much isolated. Em is definitely one of the top ten emcees of all time as far as lyrical skills go. It is no secret, though, he has been through some things that have put him on the emotional edge that was talked about in Grand Master Flash and the Furious Five's "The Message."

For a man to call a woman out of her name is far less than chivalrous. When a man pulls out those two negative terms, it is as if he is de-humanizing that particular female. I know that you know that a bitch is a female dog. Although the old adage says that a dog is a man's best friend, general consensus says that dogs are beneath humans. So, to call a woman that word is saying she isn't even the same species.

As far as the term "ho," of course over time, the spelling and pronunciation has been changed to fit the rhymes in some songs and just basically to keep up with the coolness of the times. Throughout the history of man-kind, the term "whore" has been loosely used as the lowest, most despicable, disgraceful way to describe a woman. The definition of the word whore is: a person (woman) who uses her physical being to accrue financial rewards. In every day talk: a woman who sells her body for money. Right now, we're not going to talk about the emotional afflictions a woman that does this has. But for a woman to allow a man to label her as a "whore" or "hoe" goes a long way in letting you know how that woman appreciates or lacks appreciation for herself. What threw me even more than hearing men identify women as such, was hearing women identify themselves as something so vile. I know sometimes when this is done, it is done to exert a braggadocious feel of the woman speaking of herself in the first person.

Right or wrong: A young man is in attendance at a school dance where he overhears a group of girls conversing. Jokingly, one of the girls calls another a bitch. The one in reference replies: "Ms. Bitch, to you, Ho!" A couple of songs later, the guy walks over and asks "Ms Bitch" to dance. She says "No!" As song after song is played, he walks over time after time and continues to ask her to dance. She continues to tell him "No!" The last time he comes over, she ignores him entirely. Being a young man who has not experienced rejection from the opposite sex and not knowing that this will happen to him more times than he would ever care to realize in the course of his life, he looks at her and says, "Damn, you ARE a bitch!" Now—of course she will be offended, but; does it make sense for her to be. I mean, dude just heard her refer to herself as such.

The bottom line is this: You are not now and never will be! You will not now nor will you ever give consent to a man to categorize you in such a deplorable manner! And, you, most definitely, will not classify yourself or another young lady in that respect (or lack of). EVER!!!

I love you,
Daddy

WWDS

Baby-girl,

It's time again for us to talk about priorities. You continue to see your "friends" doing this and that and you continue to ask me why can't you do some of those things. Granted, some of the things, you don't ask to do. Thank God for that. That let's me know your mom and I have instilled a sense of morality in you. That also let's me know that you have more respect for me and your mom and for yourself than some of your "friends," sad to say, have for their parents and for themselves.

Some of those things that you do ask to do, I just chalk up as teenage curiosity. Most people would label that as peer pressure. It's not that I don't subscribe to the theory of peer pressure. It's that I don't think it falls into that category until you succumb to the negative influences of certain situations. The psychological experts, more or less, use that same philosophy. You won't hear them use "peer-pressure" until something unfavorable happens. Why isn't it labeled peer pressure when someone tries to get you to do something positive? Why? Because we have a natural inclination to do good. I know we aren't all good. "For all have sinned and fallen short of the glory of God." Nevertheless, it makes us feel good to do good.

I know you have been taught right from wrong. I along with your mom did the teaching. I know in the past, you have utilized that teaching positively. Sometimes, especially in these teenage years, you see people doing things that appear to be harmless. On top of that, they look like they are having the time of their lives. Being that humans are naturally inquisitive, and being that you are a human, you are going to, from time to time wander "What would happen if I . . . ?" Being a young lady not yet on her own, and still having parents to answer to, you would serve yourself better if that question was re-phrased to "How would my parents respond if I . . . ?" And, yes! You should continue to ask yourself that question until you are paying "ALL" of your bills. Yes! That means even when you are in college. Yep, I know some college students are totally emancipated from their parents. But, most, an overwhelming majority, are still dependent on parents, grandparents or someone for most of their financial support. I suspect when you get to college, I will still be providing financial assistance. Of course, this means "Father knows best!"

I have an idea. I know you remember those once popular wristbands that read "WWJD." Those letters, of course, stood for "What Would Jesus do?" They were intended to make the wearer reflect on our savior when faced with a quandary. You think we could market some that read "WWDS?" Those letters would stand for "What Would Daddy Say?"

Now, don't think for one second that I am attempting to put earthly fathers on the level with Jesus. The savior was unblemished. We, on the other hand, are full of flaws. Most of us aren't as inconsistent as we were in our youth, though. Never the less, wearing the "WWDS" would just make the connection a little more tangible. Although, my personal belief is that those types of reminders don't have an effect on the wearer's decision when faced with a dilemma. If the wearer is a morally conscious person, she will, more times than not, tend to lean towards making the right decision anyway. Whether that is a popular decision or not, she realizes for the rest of her life, she will have to live with the choice she made. No matter how big or small, the consequences will be hers to deal with.

You know how we, from time to time, watch nature shows on TV. Do you ever remember seeing an eagle in flight on one of them? If you do, what one thing did you notice about that eagle that you don't notice when you see other birds? I know as observant as you are, you detected what I am talking about. You never see eagles flying with other eagles. Living in Arkansas, we see birds flying farther south for the winter every fall. Ducks, geese and all other type of game foul fly in large groups. The eagle, on the other hand, does everything, except for mating, by herself. I challenge you to be like that eagle.

How can you be like an eagle? No, I don't want you to literally learn how to fly. Although I do remember a time when you told me you were going to be the next Bessie Coleman, the first negro woman to earn a pilot's license. I want you to take on the characteristics of the eagle by learning to fly solo, so to speak. Learn to do stuff by yourself.

We know it is good to have the comraderie and friendship of others. It makes us feel good to be able to laugh and joke with our friends. On the other hand, when young men and ladies your age are with friends, that is when the bad things that do happen, are more likely to occur. Younger people are more likely to utilize bad judgement when they are in the company of other young people. This happens for various reasons. One is that they are trying to impress their crowd. When a teen is faced with a predicament and their friends or associates aren't in the vicinity, they are more apt to make a more moral conscience decision.

See what you did? Here we go, again: When I was in the tenth grade, getting ready for school and running late, I put on a certain pair of white tube socks. Now, what made this pair so special was the fact that one of them had a hole in it. You know I have three brothers and we were all active in sports. That meant we had a lot of white tube socks in the house. I'm not saying that was the only pair with a hole in one of them; but, since Mama Sueny did the laundry, not too many with holes were kept and placed in the sock drawer. Considering the shape this one was in, I don't know how it escaped her. Maybe it was one that one of us put back in the drawer and not the dirty-clothes hamper. Boys and some men tend to do that from time to time. Anyway, getting back to the story, just like any other mom, Mama told us to always wear clean underwear and socks without holes in them. Being late and not wanting to miss the bus, I didn't adhere to her teachings, or should I say warnings, that day.

Later that day in activity period, the sophomore boys volleyball team, made up of basketball players from the same P. E. class, were on schedule in the tournament. Our activity periods were played in front of the whole school. Needless to say, as I ran after a ball one of my teammates hit out of bounds, the shoe on the foot with the hole in the sock came off. Keep in mind that I was running after a ball that was going to land out of bounds. The relevance of that is that it took me away from the rest of my team and I was basically in plain view of everyone at Brinkley High School with every toe except the big one sticking out of my sock. Yep, I missed the ball. Being a little self-conscious (as all teens are), I was more concerned about getting that shoe back on as quickly as possible than I was about getting that ball back over the net. Now, in the scheme of things, my actions and the consequences that day were very small. One thing about it though: If I had listened and done what I had been taught to do, I could've saved myself the embarrassment of that day. I guess I should've asked myself "What would Mama say?" Also, the lesson was learned. Since that day, you have never been able to nor will you ever be able to find me with holes in my socks or underwear. As I reflect back at this very moment, maybe the consequences weren't so small. Since that happened, I don't care if the house is on fire. I will put on a pair of good socks or no socks at all.

I love you,
Daddy

Good, Bad and Ugly

Isiah 1:17
"Learn to do good!"

Tee,

The way people behave in certain situations, the things they spend their money on, their conviction to their religious beliefs and even their dedication to their education reveal where their priorities lie. You can even go as far as to consider a parent's educational course for a child. Nothing infuriates me more than to see a child about three or four years old reciting the words to popular hip-hop songs from the radio or videos. Keep in mind, that I am a fan of hip-hop. But, most of the videos made by today's artists aren't appropriate for teens. Tell me, why then, a three or four year old child is looking at the video or listening to the song in Mama's car.

I'm sorry, I lied. There is something that makes me angrier than to hear a child reciting those songs. To see a child of that age doing a popular dance and not being able to recite his ABC's, recognize his letters and sight words or count to one hundred gets to me more than anything.

I know everyone loves to have fun with their child(ren). A parent spending time with a child is one of the most beautiful sights you will ever see. It seems the younger the child is, the more fun you can have with them because they are cuter, funnier and more innocent then. Also, as the old television show said, "Kids Say The Darndest Things." I can't think of anything more fun for a parent than to be present to see their child grow mentally, physically, emotionally and spiritually. The younger the child, the more of an impact the parent has on that child's development in those areas. Tell me, what's wrong with the parent being responsible enough to take fifteen to twenty minutes a day to give that child something that will give her a certain level of confidence when she starts school. Statistics show that if a child can at least do those things I mentioned a few sentences ago, she has a greater chance of being a successful student. A successful student early on, makes for a successful student later on. (and a successful professional as an adult)

Although I am sure he was a lot funnier when he said it, a few years ago, Bill Cosby said some of the same things I am saying now. A lot of people in the African-American community became enraged that he would label us as such an apathetic people. Let me clear it up for everyone's favorite TV Dad. He was not talking about everyone in our community. Hence, not everyone in our community was bothered by his assertions. Did the things he was saying bother me? Not one bit. Why? Let me just say, "A person will say "Ouch!" only if it is their toes that are being stepped on."

The Black community always has been and always will be populated by an overwhelming majority of very decent, hard working, God-fearing individuals. That is not to say we don't have ills. Most of the letters I write you discuss those ills. Just as you will do with every other group of people, you will find the good, the bad and the ugly in our neighborhoods. Even when you do that, you will see that the good have some bad and ugly in them. The bad have some good and ugly in them. Even the ugly have some good and bad in them.

As a little boy, your grandparents taught me that there is some of this in everyone. Through life's experiences, I have found this to be accurate. The dilemma is to find out how much of each characteristic the individuals you deal with have. There is also a dilemma within you. That is to determine what kind of person the world will view you as by letting the trait you feel most important to you shine the most.

For the rest of your life, you will have to deal with people that you won't be fond of. Even more so, being an African-American female living in America, you will have to deal with people that aren't particularly fond of you. These people do not now nor will they at any point in your life, dictate your mistakes, your actions or your successes. As Eleanor Roosevelt once stated, "No one can make you feel inferior without your consent." You are a child of God. Turning to him during these times and by doing his will governs your successes. With him, there may be mistakes; but, never any failures.

I love you,
Daddy

Daddy's Lil' Girl

Proverbs 22:6
"Train up a child the way he (she) should go;
even when he (she) is old, he (she) will not depart
from it."

Cube,

You know I am always telling you that a major sign of maturity is being able to admit when you do something wrong. You must be able to accept responsibility for your actions and not place the blame elsewhere. In the adult world, it's referred to as taking ownership. Today, I have to say that Daddy has been wrong in one of the things he has been telling you these last few years.

First, let me tell you why I took the stance that I took. Through the years, I have told you millions of stories of my early childhood in Bucktown. You've heard the good and the bad. You've heard the funny and the sad. I have also told you what it was like growing up in a family of four boys with parents that did not allow the words "I" and "can't" to be uttered in the same sentence. They weren't the kinds of parents that would push a child incessantly, though. Walter and Sueney were undemanding enough to let us choose our activities. The one thing you didn't do, though, was start something and come home and say you were going to quit. Not in their house, you didn't.

This brings me to where I have been wrong. I have been telling you to not be so sensitive. A lot of times when you are faced with adversity, your initial reaction is to start crying. I wasn't raised like that and I am not used to that. I know you are at that awkward stage and I know a lot of things are going on with you inside and out. You are leaving that little girl stage. (Why, God? Not "my" little girl) Daddies everywhere fear this time. We fear it, for one, because it is something we will never fully understand. Two, because we think it takes our once innocent "Baby-girl" away from us. We don't think it takes our daughters physically. We just think the relationship that was once shared as only a father and daughter can, will be severed. No longer will we enjoy the bright-eyed laughter of what we view as our own renewed innocence. The one earthly thing we are associated with that conveys pure unadulterated righteousness will be gone forever.

That is the immature selfishness in us. In reality, we know we can't stop you from growing. Being sensible, we shouldn't want to. We should be able to enjoy you just as much as a maturing young lady as we did when we bounced you on our knee or swung you in the blanket. (No, Tee Cee, you are too old and my back is too far gone for me to be swinging you in a blanket.)

I love you,
Daddy

Sir, Yes Sir!

Leviticus 19:32
"Likewise, you who are younger, be subject to the elders."

Binti,

This past weekend at your sleepover for your fourteenth birthday, I noticed something. Whenever I asked one of your friends a question or evoked a response from them, very seldom did I get a respectful response. I'm not saying that they answered with something way out of left field. What I am saying is that unless it came from you or your cousins, Kirsten, Angel or Laila, or your best friend Alyssa, the reply was never followed with a sir. Did it offend me? No, it didn't. After it happened a few times and I began to notice, I thought about the disservice the parents of these young ladies were doing to their daughters. After meeting and talking to all of their parents, I think I would be accurate in assuming they all have just as great of a love for their daughters as I have for you. Nevertheless, they are missing a fantastic opportunity to give their children something that will benefit them immensely now and for years to come.

You and I have talked about those two little words, sir and ma'am, on several occasions. I can't find the words to express how much favor this will get you with adults. This preferentiality given is even greater today since your generation "has no respect for adults." That comes mostly from the adults who have not taught the children in their lives respect. This also comes from adults who selectively choose to forget their childhood. There have always been children who lack respect for adults. If it wasn't them, they definitely knew a "juvenile delinquent." That's what children who disrespected adults and authority were called back in the day. If a child is not taught respect, it stands to reason, that child is not going to show respect.

The usage of those two words by an adolescent carries weight in every forum you can think of. In today's school, the students who show respect in that manner, are considered the teacher's pets by the other students. The teacher, on the other hand, will view that student as someone who comes from a respectable family and from time to time may do some things for that student that wouldn't be done for other students who don't display those pleasing characteristics. Is that right for a teacher to do that? I would say "No." However, students and parents of students must realize that teachers are human. Positive actions beget positive reactions. Likewise, positive actions beget positive responses.

See what you did? Here we go, again: I know with most of today's teen-agers, to be a girl scout or boy scout is the personification of being geeky or nerdy. Well, Daddy was a scout. A cub scout and a boy scout. Now, you know your grandparents encouraged us to be respectful and utilize those two handles. Actually, before it became popular for parents to befriend their children, most parents encouraged it. The incident that made me start viewing male adults as a sir and female adults as a ma'am came from those years in the scouts. As a scout, you were required to refer to the den master as "Sir." It was somewhat reminiscent of the armed services. Well, on this particular day, one of the older boys had a brain fart while talking to our leader. Not only did he not identify him with a "Sir," he actually called him by his first name. My first response was "Dude must be high on something." I know my reaction may seem a bit over the top for the youth of today. But, you just didn't do that back then. I can still remember the way the den master spun around and looked at the assailant. I say assailant because the adult in the situation reacted as if the boy had hit him in the head with a rock or something. Now, just like in the armed forces, to teach discipline, one must be disciplined when he steps out of line. This leader's favorite disciplinary maneuver was the "belt line." To perform this, he would take all of the scouts, minus the one to be "corrected," divide them into two groups and line them up approximately three feet opposite of each other. The guilty party would be placed at either end. When given the say-so, he would run down the lane formed by his peers as fast as he could. While he was doing this, his "friends" were flogging him with their belts they had removed for the "festivities." Of course, the faster you made it through the line, the fewer licks you got. After seeing this for the first time, I promised myself that I would never do anything for me to have to be subjected to this. As I am sure you have noticed, Yes Sir, No Sir, Yes Ma'am and No Ma'am have stuck with me very tightly to this day.

I love you,
Daddy

The Closest Distance Between Two Points

Romans 5:3
"pressure produces unswerving endurance"

Tee,

I can only think of a few occasions in the past when I was as proud of you as I was yesterday. When Mama's associate and her son came over to make a presentation attempting to sell some cutlery, you handled yourself very admirably. (Like the champ I have been training for that moment) I knew when they came through the door the young man was going to ask you for your number. Like I always tell you, Daddy doesn't know everything. Daddy does, however, know how young men think. Actually, that one was incredibly easy to call. Just think about it: A descent looking fifteen year old young man teaching himself to play the piano and a very attractive fourteen year old young lady who is being formally taught to play. The two families have been loosely acquainted since you two were three and two respectively and attending your Mom's home daycare.

Baby, I know there will come a time that you will have a genuine interest in a young man. I am not and will not then try to keep you from your natural progression into womanhood. What I am doing is trying my hardest to dissuade that from coming before you get to the point where you can handle it emotionally and academically. I have seen so many young ladies (and men) with so much promise get into a relationship when they are no where near ready for it.

These life-altering relations usually end up tearing the young lady down in so many ways. I was tempted to use the word destroy. Of course, when you destroy something, there is no re-building. These "too early" relationships don't destroy the young people involved. It does take their focus from where it was before they entered it, though. The longer the relationship lasts, the longer it takes the person affected by it to recover. In looking at the recovery time, you should also consider if the relationship involved sex. Most of the time it does. Young men and women around your age, as you know, have an abundance of hormones. You are having emotional feelings that are foreign to you and your body is doing things that further take you into the unknown. This additionally expresses my point that makes this a very bad time to get involved in a relationship. Furthermore, most adolescents getting into one will be embroiled in their first. The key is not letting these feelings nor your emotions control you.

I think I would be hard-pressed to find a teenager that doesn't have an inkling of what she aspires to be when she becomes an adult. Some may have a better aim at what they are shooting for. By that, I mean they may already have narrowed it down and are completely focussed on one career choice. Others, on the other hand, may have several choices they are considering. Regardless, they all have something in mind. The easiest way to get sidetracked is to venture off into a relationship before you are ready. The easiest geometrical phrase to remember is "The closest distance between two points is a straight line." You know this is one of my favorite sayings. It can be applied to so many of life's situations. In this case, where you are at this very point in life is the starting point (point A) and your life's ambition (your family and career), is the ending point(point B). Now, you will, or at least you can, eventually reach that desired point even when you allow obstacles to alter your focus (Or for this conversation, when you get off the straight line) The quickest and easiest way to reach your goal is to travel in that straight line and not lose your focus.

I love you,
Daddy

Even If He Buys You a Prada,
He Still Gets Nada

Proverbs 31
"She (you are) is worth far more than rubies."

Tee Cee,

The other day while listening to talk radio, I heard a father talking about his daughter and her prom date. He said "Deena" became impregnated on the night of her prom. The devastated dad said when he and the mother asked their daughter if that was her first time engaging in sex, she said yes. Then they asked her if she had waited all of her high school career, what made her decide that this was the right time. He said her answer hurt every fiber of his and his wife's existence. She said she owed the guy since he took her to prom. I would assert that there are one of two reasons (or possibly both) that her reply overwhelmed them. The first is because it forced both parents to realize they failed their child by not instilling enough of a sense of pride as a young lady. The second has to do with how she views herself as a lady, as opposed to a woman, in a male-dominated society.

Throughout the conversation, they repeatedly told how Deena had her head on straight in every other segment of her life. Obviously, they had done a great job with her upbringing. So, what was the root of the problem in the prom night predicament? I say it goes back to dad. They also talked about how they would always go out as a family. Where ever and whenever they went out, it was always the three of them together. A part of that is okay. Of course it is great to spend family time. We do it all the time.

When a father has a daughter, it is his responsibility to show and teach her how a man is supposed to treat her. Do you know why if I am in town on Saturday mornings, you and Lisa get breakfast in bed? Do you know why I open the door for you or why you and I go out to eat sometimes without Mama? This is called "Dating your daughter." When you do get to the dating age, you need to know how your date should treat you. From our dates, you know that a young man should do all the small things that I have done for you over the years. He should not rush you. However, if the two of you have set a time to go out, it is common decency to be ready when he comes to pick you up. You know how I always tell you there is one thing you can almost always do: BE ON TIME. Daddy doesn't subscribe to that CPT bull. We know that stands for Colored People Time. You know I refuse to be stereotyped. Getting back to the young man, he should open doors for you. A lady (not a woman) wants, deserves and commands decorum. When eating out, he should order for you before he orders for himself. Whether it is at McDonald's or Paul Williams Steakhouse, he needs to know you expect nothing less than to be treated like he would want someone to treat his mom when she went out on a date.

I want you to know just because a man takes you out and spends money on you, you don't owe him anything. My bad! You owe him a thank you. (**nothing** more-**nothing** less) I say you don't owe him anything because it was his decision to ask you out.

Even if the date came about via the Sadie Hawkins route, you still don't "owe" him anything more than a polite "Thank You." If you are thinking because I am so old fashioned in my way of thinking that I might have problems grasping the concept of a lady asking a man out, you're somewhat correct. I think the man should be the hunter. To me, it takes away a little of that something that makes a lady a lady when she becomes the hunter. I don't know for sure, but maybe that's where the term "cougar" comes from.

The things he thinks he deserves, unh-unh. If you give him what he wants, he'll have you paying for the meal he invited you to, have you chauffeur him around in the car "I" bought or even worse, he'll have you hand him the keys so he can sport it and pick up other young ladies. We haven't even gotten to what he thinks you owe him in the physically affectionate department.

Do you owe him "at least a kiss?" That is how some young man is going to ask you. "Can I have at least a kiss?" No, you don't owe him "at least a kiss." Remember this when you hear it. I promise you with everything that I am that you definitely will hear it. Each kiss leads to another kiss, which leads to hugging, which leads to touching, which leads to sex.

You need to be aware that when you give a young man the slightest physical edge, he is going to try and push that edge as far as he can. More times than not, this gets young ladies into very uncomfortable and compromising situations. What does he get? He gets zilch, zero, naught, nil, nothing, Even if he buys you a Prada, he still gets nada.

I love you,
Daddy

Lead and Succeed or Follow and Get Swallowed

Romans 12:8
"If your gift is leadership, let him (her) lead."

Sugar-cube,

The other day we had to deal with an incident that I didn't think you and I would ever, ever have to deal with. Skipping class! Before you get to thinking that I didn't believe you when you said you weren't trying to skip, honestly, I do. So, I guess we need to talk about leading and following. You know Daddy has a saying for just about everything. This one is "Lead and Succeed or Follow and Get Swallowed."

In every thing you will ever do, you will either choose to be a leader or a follower. So far, you have been a leader in most of your endeavors. I have always been proud to know that when you are with your friends, I don't have to worry about them influencing you to take the negative route. In this last incident, I don't know if you actually followed. I do know, however, that you didn't do everything you were supposed to.

Let me explain. You will never see a successful person who is a follower. To put it short, if you choose to lead, you have a greater chance to succeed at what you do or what you are doing. Choosing the leadership role is just like anything else. The more you do it, the easier it comes to you. Also, the more you choose to follow, the easier it becomes.

A great analogy for that comes from mother-nature. Think about the great African lion. He's the king of the jungle. Actually, the analogy comes from one of the lion's favorite prey in the African Savannah: the wilderbeast. In looking at films of the lion stalking the wilderbeast herd, you will never see the lions attack the front of the herd. For this conversation, let's refer to the front of the herd as the leaders. In reality, they *are* leading the herd. Where does the lion attack. Every time, the lion attacks the herd, it's from the rear. We will refer to the rear as the followers. Why? Because, they are following. Why do they attack the followers? The lions instinctively know that the leaders of the herd are the strongest, fastest and smartest. They also know that in attacking these, they would be in for more of a fight. The followers definitely make for an easier target. In the attack, the lions will actually allow the leaders to pass them as they sit back in waiting for the followers.

Sometimes, you will see one of the lions kill one of the young. That doesn't mean all of the young are weak and followers. When in the presence of other youth, there are some that will lead and some that will follow. When in the presence of adult humans, just as with the widerbeast, youth do, in fact, become followers. Why? The more experienced adults are stronger mentally, physically and emotionally. If the herd is not running, you will see some of the young in the midst of the pack and not always at the back.

Of course, the young of the herd symbolizes you. Being young, I know you think you know everything. You believe if you had to, you could fend for yourself. Trust me, I admire that in you. But, as the Fat Boys said back in the day "Don't Be Stupid." Our perverse, demented society has people in it that will chew you up and spit you out without staining their teeth.

The Bible references the Devil as a hungry lion going to and fro seeking whom he may devour. Believe me, the Devil is smarter and more cunning than any of us could ever dream of being. I'm talking about the leaders and the followers of all mankind. As I have told you many times before, the devil attacks us all at our weakest points. He is shrewd enough to know everybody's. Still, I contend, he, just like the lions of Africa, chalks up more kills when he attacks the followers than he does when he attacks the leaders.

I love you,
Daddy

A Beautiful You

I Samuel 25: 32-42
"Abigail: A beautiful woman with a beautiful mind"

Figlio,

You know everything about me is ol' skool, right. My conversation is about back in the day and almost all of the music I listen to is seriously out-dated. For the record, my music intelligence goes back farther than the inception of rap in the boroughs of New York City. Although I was born in the middle of the Motown invasion, I know and love all of the tunes and compositions of that era just as much as I love rap and hip-hop. You probably know all the words just as well as I do, though. You remember the family trips when it was my turn to occupy the CD player or on the road late at night when everyone else was asleep.

One of my favorite groups of all time is the Temptations. I dare anyone to suggest a group from any genre of music from any era that could harmonize as well as or better than the Temps. One song I don't agree with that the Temps sang is "Beauty's Only Skin Deep." Yes, I know it's just the title of a song. There is an old saying that says "If a lie is told enough, it becomes the truth." Case in point: the public perception of beauty.

I recall a few years ago, you came home upset that, your now best friend, Mckayla made reference to your darker skin color. Of course she is a very lighter skinned young lady. I remember it like it was yesterday. It's funny how some things just have the tendency to stay strong in our memories. I guess this one stays in mine because it is a day that I knew would come. Even with my constant drilling into your psyche that beauty comes in all shapes sizes and colors, when you see basically the same type of woman on TV or when you thumb through fashion magazines, I knew you would eventually question what I was trying to instill in you. Please believe me when I say that a woman that takes care of herself mentally, physically, emotionally and spiritually has already defeated the belief that all beautiful women are cut from the same cookie cutter. They also aren't created with the same kind or colored dough.

This is what Tyra Banks is trying to teach the young ladies of the world. You can't help but admire her for what she did to revolutionize the fashion industry. She forced the designers, magazines, TV and Hollywood to finally recognize the beauty in women that don't fit into their microscopic panorama of beauty. She forced them to realize there are some beautiful women with curves. Most women do have curves and a lot of the designs you see on the fashion runways wouldn't fit them right. On top of doing that, she has proven to be a very, very astute business woman.

Having majored in radio-tv in school, I have always been a fan of talk-radio. I never really was a fan of television talk shows until I started listening to what Tyra was saying to today's young ladies. Of course having a teen daughter that is dealing with or will deal with some of the same topics confronted on Tyra's show sort of pulled me in.

With society being so deviant and men still claiming ownership of the world, young ladies and girls your age need someone to tell them they are beautiful. Ideally, I think this should come from their fathers. To come from a young lady that has a knack in relating to them and has done some of the things she has done offers a pleasing alternative, though.

In nature, the peacock is supposed to be one of the most picturesque creatures God made. I can remember one time when we took the family to the zoo and you made a comment about a peacock's tail. This point of view comes from mankind, of course. Tell me how we can see the difference in these birds and still label them as beautiful, yet can't see beauty in women that are different than those the media hold as the epitome of feminine elegance? Just like no two peacocks eyes on their tails are the same, no two women are the same. Every woman has her own distinct look and if she takes pride in that look and nurtures it, she is a beautiful creature. She can be of any race. She can be thin or thick. She can also be short or tall. She can have very full lips or she can have very thin lips. She can have a big butt or she can have that dreaded disease "noassatall." She doesn't necessarily have to be at least 5'9" between 115-135lbs. As B.O.B. sang in his song Beautiful Girl, "They got nothing on you, Baby!"

Being a man that tries to be honest with himself, I can't hold those views against the media. Most media outlets are owned in large part by white males. Going back to the peacock: What bird looks good to a male peacock? A female peacock, right? To most white men, what woman looks best to them? A white woman, right? Being totally honest, a black woman that takes care of herself in the ways spoken of above, is the most beautiful creature on earth to me. That is not to say I don't think there aren't beautiful women of other races. You might even say it's the vanity that is in all of us. We are attracted to people that are like us. It doesn't have to be in the physical realm, though. If you were to poll all the patrons of the successful online dating services, you will see that they are looking for someone that they have something in common with. Take me and your mom: I have been told by several people that we could pass for siblings. From the first time I saw her, I have always thought she was one of the most beautiful women I have ever laid eyes on. I told my dad on our wedding day that she was, in fact, the most beautiful woman on earth.

Since I first began to notice females with the interest of the opposite sex, it always puzzled me as to why some types of women were never seen as beautiful by the media outlets. One thing you didn't see when I was growing up in small town Arkansas was a black woman on the evening news. Did that mean black women couldn't earn college degrees that would allow them to pursue news anchor careers? No, I don't think that was it. I think they were using common sense. Since it was a given that blacks weren't going to be hired in the small southern markets, why would they waste their time seeking a degree that they could not utilize when everything was said and done. Growing up, I had several black teachers that were very well-spoken and had that pleasant trusting look stations look for. Of course, the ladies in our communities that had the opportunity to go to college were encouraged to go into teaching. They could always get a job because good teachers are always in constant demand.

Earlier in this letter, I talked about Tyra Banks. I would be seriously remiss if I didn't mention the lady that started it all for "different" looking ladies on television. Of course I'm talking about that power house Oprah Winfrey. What was her contribution? All she did was show us that a black woman with black facial features can deliver the ratings in a larger media market. How ironic is it that she did this in the largest city in our nation that was founded by a black man. In case you didn't know, Jean-Baptist-Point Du Sable, a black pioneer and trader, founded Chicago.

As for Oprah, she first accomplished this on a regional level by taking the Chicago market. In my opinion, this was the most important step she made. When young ladies can see someone in their community making a difference, I think it carries a lot more weight than when they see someone who has achieved the status she has today. At that point, some people have become a little detached from the community and the people see them as larger than life stars rather than people. This is not to say that she has become detached, nor is it meant to devalue her recent accomplishments by any means. If she was, she wouldn't have given to the global community the contributions she has. Financially, she is helping more people than she ever would have been able to if she had stayed regional.

A lot of people won't believe it when I say this. To help others is one of the main reasons we were put here. "Are you your sister's keeper? Yes, you are!"

I love you,
Daddy

Life

(The poem)

I Timothy 6:18
" . . . do good . . . be willing to share."

Sometimes, our life takes us places we never intended to go

Question—fast or slow
Answer—yes or no
Never throw—someone you love below (the bus)

Lust—never
Fuss—hardly ever
Dust, the skeletons (from your closet daily)

Nearly—miss
Dearly—kiss
Clearly, love hurts! (from time to time)

Do—chores
Few—stores
New, stuff eventually bores (you to death)

Crime—never pays
Shine—all your days
Rhyme—today's rap craze
Time, is a commodity (you can't afford to waste)

Give—love
Forgive—beloved
Live, not above (your means)

Trif-ling, never be as a mother
Strife—not to your sisters or brothers
Life, was given to us (for us to give back to others)

> I love you,
> Daddy

Work Hard Now, Play Harder Later

Colossians 3:23
"Whatever you do,
work it with all your heart . . ."

Baby-Girl,

As you know, Cooley High is one of my favorite movies of all time. When I was a teen-ager, it was my favorite. One of the scenes from it had the teacher, Mr. Mason, talking to Preach. Preach and his friend Cochese had benefitted from the teacher's friendship with a local police officer and was released from jail after having been picked up for joy riding with a couple of local hoods. Frustrated with Preach, yet knowing his intelligence and the promise his future held, Mr. Mason made those points to him and told him that with an education, he could have anything he wanted. Then he asked him isn't there anything he wanted out of life. Sarcastically, Preach replied, "Yea, I want to live forever." As if to ask, "Can an education help me live forever?"

No! An education can't help you to live forever. Nothing on earth can make you live forever. I will say that an education can get you just about anything short of immortality, though. Taking your education as far as you are mentally capable of will, more than anything, give you a feeling of accomplishment that you can't get from too many other endeavors. It also will give you the understanding skill and confidence to excel at whatever career choice you made. Pursuing it all the way will allow you to provide a comfortable living for yourself and, later in life, for your family.

Do you remember the fable of the ant and the grasshopper? The ant worked and worked storing up food for the winter. The grasshopper, on the other hand, frolicked his time away during the easy comfortable season, when he should have been preparing for life in the lean season when the good things weren't so plentiful. I know you know by now Daddy is going to have a way to relate this to the topic at hand.

You and most young ladies need to take the stance the ant took. Look at it like this. You are in the comfortable season of your lives. Your parents or whoever your legal guardians are, provide for you just as mother-nature provided for the ant. Just as the ant took advantage of the favorable conditions, you need to take advantage now when your only job is school. Again, like the ant, you need to "work hard now, so you can play harder later." The antithesis, or exact opposite, of this is "play hard now, and work harder later."

Working hard at this point in your life at least gives you the opportunity to make a decision on what you want to do with your life. It opens up countless possibilities that you won't even have the chance to consider without the hard work you put into school. I promise you that the lady who worked hard and gave herself the opportunity to choose a career is having more fun on a daily basis than the lady who didn't work hard in school and ended up having to settle for a job that doesn't coincide with her personality or how she likes to spend her time. The lady mentioned in the latter part of the sentence works to give her family the necessities. The lady mentioned in the former, works to give her family a nice comfortable existence. I also promise you something else. If you work hard in school and afford yourself those opportunities, you will make more money at a job or career you like than you would at one you don't.

Who do you think would have the money to travel with their family and have a more enjoyable vacation, a professional person who worked hard and got their college degree or someone who didn't work hard in junior high and high school, thus denying themselves the opportunity to go to college and secure an occupation that would provide affluently.

Your most important work at this point in your life is school. Even for those young ladies that have to work to help support their families, school is still the most important job for them right now. The only way to get out of their current situation is to get a good education.

Having gone to college and having worked in law enforcement, I have friends and associates that range from CEO's to surgeons to janitors to crack dealers. In evaluating these men, I would have to say the biggest difference would have to be their educational level. I say that because some of the M.D.'s grew up in the same neighborhood under the same socio-economic circumstances as some of the drug dealers and drug abusers. What separated them? What made one choose to get out of the gutter and the other wallow in it? Baby, Daddy doesn't have an answer to that. I can tell you that those who chose to get out and have a better life for himself and his family was either told or figured out for themselves that education was the best and sometimes the only way.

I say most young ladies need to take the stance of the ant because, sad to say, not all children have someone looking out for their welfare. Those that do, should consider it a true blessing to have someone that hasn't let the ills of the world (drugs and other things) affect their judgment in providing and caring for them. I take that back. All of the young ladies your age need to take that stance. It may be harder for some that don't have the support structure that you and some of your friends have. Still, everyone in school must realize "The future depends on the now." For those that don't have this, I sincerely pray nightly for them. You, my dear, fall into the category of the "haves." To whom much is given, much is expected. Keep that and let it marinate.

I love you,
Daddy

Move Somethin'
(exercise)

Proverbs 17:22
"A cheerful heart is good medicine."

Musume,

You have been really grouchy these past couple of days. What's going on? I know. Do You? What's going on is that since cheerleader practice began, the workouts have been taking its toll on you. Why? Because you didn't prepare yourself for it. You have to keep your body in tune for what you are preparing to use it for. Simply put, you have to exercise regularly.

Exercising regularly will do so much for you, inside and out. A young lady that exercises regularly will be more attractive to young men. It also helps you by keeping your muscles tight and also by giving you the confidence to "know" you are looking right. Now, don't confuse confidence with conceit. To be confident in yourself is to realize you have done what it takes to give you the edge in whatever situation you are about to take on. Conceit, on the other hand, is to have an exaggerated sense of one's self. A confident young lady will be able to perform well after she and her team advances to the finals of the cheerleading competition. (why is it called a competition if "they" say cheering isn't a sport) A conceited young lady will expect the judges to award her team with the first place trophy because she is so cute and her outfit fits so well.

One thing I am happy about you and your exercise regimen is that you aren't one of your age group's game-heads. You never have been one of those kids who likes to stay in the house and play games. I like the fact that you like outdoor games. One of the hottest topics about children today is the fact that they don't like to go outside and play any more. This has brought about a more over weight average American child. This, in turn, has brought about more children being diagnosed with childhood diabetes.

See what you did? Here we go again: When I was about six or seven years old, I remember one time it rained for about three days straight. Your uncle Corey and I had grown tired of being inside. Although we had each other and the dog to play with, we had always been little boys who wanted to be outside. Where were your uncles Garland and Prep? Well, even when we were little boys, Garland always did his own thing and Prep hadn't been born yet. I'm guessing the day I am going to tell you about was a Saturday. I say that because your Grandma wasn't at work, your Grandpa was at work and we hadn't gone to church. After having grown totally tired of the rain keeping us inside, we devised a plan to get out of the house. Basically, all we did was wait for your Grandma to go to sleep. It must have been during one of the warmer months because I recall all we put on were some baseball caps and the slickest jackets we could find. We didn't have money for raincoats. Thinking back, we probably put on some of those old "pleather" jackets. I know you don't know anything about "pleather." That is a material that looks like leather but is actually closer to plastic.

After concocting our diabolical plan, we waited for her to fall asleep. When she did, we headed for the door not realizing Donut, the dog, was tired of being confined to the inside also. Of course, having him outside in the rain with us made it that much more fun. I remember us having so much fun playing outside in the rain with that dog. It seemed like we had been out there all evening before Mama woke up, realized we weren't in the house and called us in. Of course, we knew when we first started constructing the plan it would end with us getting a whuppin'. Although I remember us making plans to get out of the house, I can't remember us planning to come back. I guess we planned on playing until she called us in. Subconsciously, we had already considered the consequences and repercussions. Yet, to be able to go outside for that little bit of time must have been worth it. That mentality of having to be outside playing took us on to be pretty good athletes with wanting to exercise engrained in us even today.

A few years back, you asked me "Daddy, why do you exercise all the time?" I remember telling you "To keep

Daddy feeling good." A lot of people don't realize it. Exercise actually does make you feel good. To give you a little lesson in health-science, the body does this by releasing endorphins into the body. They are produced by the pituitary gland and the hypothalamus when you do some serious strenuous exercising. They act as natural pain relievers and offer an increased sense of euphoria. In every day language, it acts as somewhat of a drug. Morphine, to be exact. This is what is in effect when a person is running and experiences the "runner's high." Anyone that exercises, using any method, will tell you that you don't necessarily have to be a runner to experience the "high."

Remember, when you get to feeling down or you get to feeling like you are losing that shape you are so proud of, ask your dad to put you together a work out. In time, you will be able to do it for yourself. What ever the case, make sure you continue to move somethin'.

I love you,
Daddy

"I'm Sorry?"

Matthew 18:21-22
"How many times shall I forgive . . .
seventy times seven."

Tochter,

"Daddy, why can't some people tell other people they have hurt, that they are sorry?" Just like some other questions you ask me, Baby, Daddy doesn't know the answer to that one. Daddy thinks that it must be something in their past experiences that make it difficult to say those two little words. If I remember correctly, we were taught in kindergarten to apologize.

Some of these people that can't say it have been hurt mentally, physically or emotionally. Some have suffered all of the abuse you can dream of. Sometimes, young people your age have seen someone else go through abuse or maltreatment of some kind. For a child to see a parent, or both parents, go through this can be as damaging as going through it themselves. To go through this type of mistreatment sometimes forces the victim to build imaginary walls. Once this wall is up, the person thinks it makes them weak or vulnerable to say, "I'm sorry."

Know this: Everybody makes mistakes. There has only been one person that walked the face of the earth that didn't make mistakes. Truth be told, he wasn't 100% human. He had to be God in human form to be able to not make mistakes. Notice I didn't say "Everybody makes *a* mistake." We all make mistakes over and over. To paraphrase a line from The Human League's song from 1986, "We're only human, of flesh and blood we're made. We're only human, born to make mistakes."

Making mistakes doesn't make you weak. Nor does it make you a bad person. What makes you a bad person is not being able to acknowledge your mistake, take ownership of your actions, apologize and move on. It's as simple as that. "I messed up and I'm sorry for it." Depending on the size of the "mess up," it may take more words than that. All in all though it boils down to the same thing. "I messed up and I'm sorry for it. Can we move past this?" Most people, no matter how angry they are with you, will accept your apology, eventually. Don't think they are going to immediately forget the situation that brought about their anger, though. It takes most people time to get over things.

Let me say this: It is not your job to coerce them into accepting your admission of guilt. It is your job to admit to it and ask their acceptance of your admission of guilt. It is their job to forgive. You need to expect that if you ever have the need to apologize to a friend or a foe, it may take time. If that time ever comes and you need to know how to go about it or how to say it, you know I'll be here for you.

Right now, I need to say "I am sorry" to you for something I did the other day. The other day when you, Lisa and I got home from eating out, as always, I went to open the door. You and Lisa noticed the sound of a locust. Being totally honest, I didn't notice it. Growing up in the country, I am used to those sounds. You know your mom grew up in the country, also. The fact that she is a little afraid of them, makes her take notice of the sound. When the two of you brought it to my attention that the locust itself was, ironically, on the security door, I opened the door to allow you to run in. Lisa took advantage of the door being open and ran in. You kept saying that you weren't coming in and wanted me to come get you. I actually thought you were joking like you sometimes do. You know how you sometimes just want to be babied by "Daddy." I thought this was one of those times. After telling you repeatedly to come in, I became frustrated and raised my voice. I was wrong on two occasions in this situation. First, I was wrong, as a father, not being able to recognize that you, a young lady that always has and always will, until she takes a husband, look to me for protection, was genuinely afraid. Second, I was wrong for raising my voice. In a situation in which someone is losing their poise, the last thing they need is for the person they are looking to for help, to lose theirs. That evening I took ownership of my actions, acknowledged my mistake and apologized. Since then, we have moved on.

Does my apology from that evening or the one I just gave you, make me a weak person? No! Does it make me a bad father? No, I don't think so. Like I said, if there is anything in this situation that could posssibly take some of my "Good Daddy" points, it would be the fact that I didn't recognize that you really were scared.

One thing children need to realize is that parents don't have all the answers and are going to, from time to time, not handle certain circumstances the way they should be handled. The key is to understand that every day is a new day for us too. Just like with a child, each new day brings about new adventures/situations for the parent. Unlike with the child, the parent should, from years of experience, be able to process what is happening from a proactive rather than a reactive perspective. As I said, this doesn't happen sometimes. When it doesn't, realize we make mistakes. Accept our apology and move on.

I love you,
Daddy

Keep "Those Folks" Out

Matthew 22:21
"Render unto Caesar what is Caesar's . . ."

Fille,

You and I have always been able to talk about anything that was age appropriate for you. A lot of parents don't buy into that philosophy. Why? I don't know. The only thing I can come up with at this moment is because they think it will put some negative things on the child's mind that wasn't there before. In defense to that, you know when you and I do talk about something, (especially something you haven't experienced yet) it is discussed in its entirety. We discuss the pros and the cons of the situation. We also talk about how everything you do in life will ultimately have a positive or a negative effect in the scheme of things. I offer you the opportunity to present your view and I, of course, present my view. If the two views differ that much, you know we converse even further.

Having said that, it brings me to this. Over the years, you have seen your older brothers in their dealings with law enforcement and the courts. A lot of the things they are dealing with, still today, could have been avoided. *ALL* of them could have been avoided. The average person will, from time to time, get a traffic ticket, though. You know how your Daddy does things. So, you know as they were growing up, your Daddy told them how to avoid those things.

Having been in law enforcement, I have seen what a bad cop can do. With them being young black men, I gave them instructions, almost on a daily basis, on how to avoid coming in contact with the bad cops. I also instructed them on what to do if, by some unfortunate event, they did come into contact with a bad cop. They were told what to say in certain situations, how to say it and what disposition to display.

Now, it is on you. I'm sure you have heard the old adage, "A fool can learn from his own mistakes. A wise man learns from the mistakes of others." Even with them receiving training from a father with law enforcement in his background, your brothers, Jonathon and Reggie, made mistakes. I can say that they waited until they were out on their own before those mistakes were made, though. Regardless, what I am telling you is, just like anything else in life, police officers come in good and bad. When confronted with the latter, you need to know how to deal with it.

The most important insight in this is knowing how to tame your temper. You, like your Daddy, are a very easy-going person. For the most part, you don't let too many things get to you or get you riled. This will help you immensely when you are detained for the first time. You are going to be a little scared and your first instinct will be to "call Daddy." Any officer worth his badge will offer a teenager the opportunity to contact her parents. Some won't. Remember, there are "bad cops" out there.

As a young lady, the first thing that needs to come to your mind if it is night time, when you see those lights behind you is to "get to a well lit, well populated area." As a young black lady, some officers will expect you to have a negative sassy attitude. When he comes up to the car and you hit him with, "Sir, what's seems to be the problem," you have just won the first battle. The next battle is won when the other person in the car with you displays the same composure.

I say "other person" as opposed to "other people," because as we have talked about many times before, when you drive without an adult in the car with you in your teen years, you will have no more than one other teenager riding with you. Yes, you are going to hear it again. The chance of a crash occurring increases thirty percent for every teenager in a car not accompanied by at least one adult. Sad to say, you just experienced this with the death of your cheer partner, Chelsea. This is because of the distractions that each added "friend" brings. "Yes!" You are still getting a two-seater.

Every time you add a portion of pleasantry to ease the officers mind which will in turn ease your mind, you chalk up another battle. The war is won when you leave the situation knowing you have done something, no matter how minute or gargantuan, to negate the stereotypical view of a "bad cop."

Getting back to "those folks." As I said, most people will eventually be pulled over on a routine traffic stop. This is understandable. What isn't understandable is getting "those folks" in your business under conditions more intense than this. (drugs, murder, robbery . . .) "Once you are in their system, you don't come out." Even though some courts expunge records, you still don't ever truly come out. This, over the course of time, can have a very negative effect on your professional career.

The other day, I bought a copy of one of those magazines that publish offenders pictures and what they are being charged with. Now I regret that I bought it. I will never buy another one or any magazine like it. These types of magazines aren't fair to some of the people that appear in them. Our laws say "innocent until proven guilty." Most of the people in these types of magazines have only been detained and haven't been to court.

Several years back, I probably would've been in one of them. I had a mug shot taken because of a warrant issued resulting from someone committing identity theft against me. Would that have been fair for my picture to be placed in there?

Another reason you don't want to be involved with "those folks" is that it drains you dry financially. The court systems are all about money. The jails are all about money. The prisons are all about money. The only way they can continue to operate is to continue to get "our" money or to get government monies from keeping "us" locked up. I say "us" because we are disproportionately locked up. It's a business. The key is to keep "those folks" out of *your* business.

I love you,
Daddy

Teen Sex

1 Thessalonians 4:3

" . . . avoid sexual immorality."

Cutie,

When I picked you up from cheer camp the other day, you were really excited that the girls from last year's squad came by to visit. Now that I think about it, you seemed to be more excited by the talk that your aunt and uncle gave the visiting girls. With your aunt being the sponsor for the cheer squad, I guess she felt compelled to impart some of her womanly experience to those young ladies heading off to college. To have an older, more mature, more experienced lady teaching younger ladies is always a good thing. It is also a good thing when having a discussion like this, to have an older male give a man's perspective and let the young ladies know how a younger man thinks. When the conversation involves sex, it is invaluable for young ladies to hear from the opposite sex. As animated as your uncle is, I am sure he said some things you and the other young ladies will never forget.

In telling me about the talk and the girls, you mentioned one of the young ladies was pregnant and didn't know if she was going to be able to go to college like all of her friends were going to do. There are some big detractors to ladies your age having sex, but I feel safe saying that pregnancy is the biggest. I say this because a female, no matter what age, has a lot to deal with while being pregnant. There is a lot to cope with physically and emotionally. If some adult females find it hard to handle, just think how difficult it is for expectant teen mothers.

Before I continue, let me point out a major distinction. The young ladies that were the focus of their talk, were heading off to college. I'm guessing they ranged in age anywhere from seventeen to nineteen. I know you don't want to believe it now, but, there are enormous differences in a seventeen year old and a fourteen year old. There are differences in seventeen year olds and nineteen year olds as well. The differences in fourteen year olds and nineteen year olds are almost as plentiful as the differences between a toddler and a teen. This can pertain to young ladies and men. Two of the most clear cut differences are the same ones I mentioned earlier that make it easier for an older lady to endure a pregnancy versus a younger lady your age.

Considering the physical aspect of a pregnancy, older ladies' bodies are simply more "baby-ready" than the body of their younger counter-parts. On an episode of The Tyra Show that dealt with teen pregnancy, a mother of one of the teens explained how after having a child at fifteen, her daughter's body reacted very strangely. If

I remember correctly, she said her daughter, who was in good health before the pregnancy, was chronically fatigue and began to have problems with her lower womanly parts. Her menstrual cycle, which came like clockwork before, had become impossible to predict. The length of time it stayed started to vary, too. Finally, whereas she had a normal flow previously, now the flow was quite abundant. Of course, I am not a doctor. Still, I would guess it's never good to lose blood in vast amounts. She also said the teenager whined that her body was in constant pain. Now, obviously, this isn't indicative of every teen pregnancy. It does, however, show some of the negative physical consequences that can derive from getting pregnant at an early age before your body is ready and capable of handling a child.

Let's imagine a young lady your age just had a baby and all of the negative repercussions from the last paragraph had taken place. If it were possible for the physical implications to be the only damaging effects, she would be able to take the easy route. In the real scheme of things, that is totally unfeasible. Some of the emotional is brought about by the physical.

You and I have discussed how a female's body changes during the gestation period. An older woman, in most cases, is more familiar with and more knowledgeable in the changes her body will undergo. This allows her to cope with the changes better. A teen, on the other hand, has a lot going on with her body even without being pregnant. We chat often about what adolescence does to your body. I truly would hate to be a young lady, or just as much, hate to see you going through adolescence and a pregnancy at the same time.

From time to time, you demonstrate how the physical can overwhelm the emotional without even knowing that is what you are doing. You know those times when you come to me complaining about your stomach getting big when you get lazy in your training? What do I say every time? "You'll be okay. Just lay off of the pizza and french fries." That is definitely the body having an effect on the psyche'. This is just through the normal adolescent stage that all teens go through. Young men go through adolescence, too. The difference in theirs and yours, of course, has to do with those things called hormones. (testosterone in the males and estrogen in the females) As I have told you so many times before, I am not a doctor, but, I sincerely believe this is what makes up the difference in the psychological composition of men and women.

In a teenage pregnancy, the mental or emotional can affect the physical, also. I can only imagine the thoughts that an expectant teen mother has. I don't know why, but, when most people are going through a crisis emotionally, they aren't inclined to be as concerned about their physical presence like they normally are. Yes, a teen mother, I don't care how affluent or supportive her family is, at some point in time, will find herself in crisis mode. This brings about another negative. It is very important for a female to exercise during pregnancy. In most cases, it won't result in a life or death situation. Still, going back to those endorfins, they help tremendously with dealing with the stress. Exercise also helps with the expected weight gain and with the nutritional exchange between the mother and child.

Another harmful aspect of being an expectant teen is working in partnership with the "baby daddy." You have seen and I have seen that this normally doesn't go the route that would be conducive to the upbringing of the child. To put it plainly, the teen parents routinely end up going separate ways and not as friends. A lot of the time, the parents don't even end up cordial towards one another. This happens for various reasons. You can chalk it up to fear, uncertainty or even commonness in the fact that some teens have friends or acquaintances that are in the same situation.

A lot of the young ladies and young men have tendencies to listen to friends with children. It seems as if most of the guys are looking for someone to reinforce their thoughts of not having to be a responsible parent. Some of the young ladies, on the other hand, listen to their friends who have been abandoned with a child. They take heed when they are told to make him pay. Is this a bad thing? Of course it isn't. Sometimes (not that often), but, sometimes a young lady will have a young man that wants to take ownership of his actions and actually act as a father and not as just a "baby daddy." The younger the expectant parents to be are, the harder it will be for them to psychologically handle sex, which may result in pregnancy.

I really feel for the young ladies that have to put up with a "baby daddy" that questions if the baby is his.

After DiNA tells him it is his offspring, a lot of the "baby daddy's" then choose to not have anything to do with the mother or the child. Young ladies need to remember that this is the same "boy" that told you "We need to take it to the next level." Or maybe he told you "If you love me, you would." When you are approached with these as well as many others, Daddy says—"If you have to ask yourself if the two of you are ready, then you're not."

It all boils down to one thing. No matter how you look at it, "Young teens aren't emotionally ready for parenthood."

Let's change the channel and talk about another concern regarding teen sex. On a semi-regular basis, I show you reports and articles regarding teen sex. Depending on what reports you accept as factual, you will either believe it is on the rise or on the demise. Regardless, if teens are engaging in more sex or not, it is a fact that your generation has more of a price to pay when the conversation turns to diseases. Back in the day, of course there were diseases. We didn't have the killer-type that your generation has to consider today, though. As Prince said, "The big disease with the little name," has reached epidemic proportions. You have heard the song, so you know his Purple Highness was referring to AIDS (Acquired Immune Deficiency Syndrome). AIDS is alluded to, by those not in-the-know, as the Gay disease. The crazy thing about that is the segment of the population that is being affected disproportionately is young African-American females under the age of twenty-eight.

There are several other issues we can reflect upon concerning teens having sex. The last one I want to discuss is something you can never get back, your reputation. When I tell you that the girls' names that are having sex, get around, you better know it as well as you know you have ten fingers and ten toes. Just like you and your girlfriends talk about guys, the guys talk about you and your friends. Like I tell you all the time, guys your age are being driven by their hormones.

One of the worst things I can think of about being a female teen is the fact that even if you aren't one of those females that "put out," you can still be labeled as one. Why? One of the reasons guys will unjustly identify girls that "don't" as those that "do" starts with the way some of the girls dress. Guys will treat you in the manner they perceive you. This, in itself, is odd and unfair of the young men who prematurely label young ladies. A young man will wear his pants hanging off his butt but swear up and down that he's not thugging. The same young man will, in the same breath, unjustly brand a young lady as loose. We have talked about all of this before. You know your reputation is as fragile as my bones are getting as I get older. The terrifying thing about your reputation is that once it is damaged, it is virtually impossible to reverse the affects. Once again, if you want to be treated like a lady, carry yourself like a lady.

Yesterday, when we got ready to go out to eat as a family, you asked if you could invite McKayla. After going to pick her up and reaching the restaurant, the conversation quickly turned to McKayla's boyfriend.

As we sat there discussing what made him a boyfriend versus a friend, she candidly admitted that her mom had gotten angry with her because her mom thought she saw them kiss as she arrived to pick her up after a school function. She said they actually hadn't kissed at that time. Although, she did disclose that since then, they have kissed several times. I know you remember me telling her that each time they lock lips, they get closer and closer to having sex. Your mom, of course, was of the same opinion and voiced it to McKayla. Then McKayla said, "My grandma told me the same thing." She seemed shocked that she would get the same response from people that have never met and, as far as she knows, the only thing we have in common is the acquaintance of her. Know this: most adults have been through the things you, as a teen, are going through. If you talk to ten responsible adults, you may get the story from ten different directions. Still, you will receive the same information. Remember: That is when you are talking to responsible adults.

The thing you need to take to heart is that you are still young. A relationship, especially one involving sex, is way out of the realm of you engaging in and being able to keep your focus on your lifelong dream. It throws a huge monkey wrench into a positive future.

I love you,
Daddy

The Boogey (Wo)man

James 3:16
"For where jealousy exists, there will be disorder
and every vile practice."

Angel,

All my life, I have heard female after female criticize each other. I mean from elementary school on through my high-school years, in college and into my adult life, I have witnessed first hand and through the grape vine, different girls, young ladies and full grown women talk about each other like they had absolutely no love or respect for the other.

What makes this even more unpleasant is the next time you see one of them in the presence of the person you just heard them talking about, they act like they have just run into a friend that had been lost at sea for years on a deserted island. If you were standing anywhere close to the two ladies, this is probably something like the conversation you would hear from the one you heard talking about the other one earlier. "Girl, where you been? I haven't' seen you in forever. You know you still looking good though. I wish I could'a kept my figure after I had my baby like you did. And, Girl, I really like those boots." But, truth be told, this is what she was actually thinking, "Damn, here come this skank. Why do I always have to run into her? Looking like a ol' heifer. And she know she wrong for wearing those boots—running over like a out of control eight-teen wheeler."

No, Daddy doesn't know why women treat each other like that. But, of course, I'm going to tell you why I think they do.

It can all be summed up in eight simple letters, J-E-A-L-O-U-S-Y. And a lot of the times, the woman with the 'tude doesn't have a reason to be jealous.

A lot of times, women tend to be jealous when they subconsciously feel they are lacking in certain areas of their lives. Actually, I think this is the reason for the envy you find in most people. (women or men) They can feel inadequate physically, emotionally or in lots of other areas and instead of addressing those issues, they turn their inner feelings toward someone else.

Oh, before I continue, earlier I mentioned seeing girls talking about each other when I was in elementary school. I think this makes my case in saying that jealousy is a learned behavior. Correct me if I am wrong. But, little girls in elementary school don't naturally know enough to be jealous of other little girls. At least not to the point of talking about them behind their backs. I think they become skilled at this while listening to the older females in their lives talking about their own acquaintances. Take note, I didn't say "Talking about their own friends." "You don't talk about your friends."

If you are handling your business, you have no reason to feel envious of ANYONE else. If you know, without a doubt, that you are on point when it comes to your physical (your body), your mental (your grades), your spiritual (your God) and your emotions (your psyche'), you truly have no need to sit back and demean another female. If you have all those things together, you won't have or feel that you have the need to degrade someone else. To go even deeper, when you see a lady that is secure with herself, you will more than likely see just the opposite. You will see a lady that can and will find the good in others. And if she is really secure, she will point out and make it known the good she notices in other people.

Just for the record, men can be jealous of other men, too. But, just like women, when you see a man secure in himself, he will respond just like the self-assured female.

Another thing that I find peculiar is how a lot of grown women will say they don't have many female friends. "I just hang out with the guys." I consider myself a level-headed individual, so, take this from a level-headed guy. Guys don't like to hear this.

Also, I think women not having many, if any, female friends comes from that jealousy thing. But, I can say that when you find a lady with a good friend, they are almost inseparable. Take Oprah and Gayle's friendship for instance. That is one to be admired.

While you are growing up, if you are blessed enough to find a female friend and the two of you nurture that friendship you will be very fortunate. And when I say friendships, I'm talking about a friend that is as close to you as a sister.

You won't find many people who have lifelong friendships. I sincerely believe they are works of art that should be treasured.

I love you,
TC

Don't Get Caught In The Net

Galatians 5:19

"Now the works of the flesh are evident . . ."

Kirstin,

The other day when we were at the mall, I noticed how happy you were when you ran into your fifth grade classmate, Autumn. Both of your faces lit up and you hugged each other and acted like you would never see each other again.

Now, you know anything positive and genuine that makes you happy makes me happy. Parents love to see their children enjoying themselves. One of the brightest spots of my day is when I get the opportunity to see you smiling or laughing. Why does it make me happy to see you happy? Simply put: When you love someone, you love to see them happy.

Let me get back to my reason for writing this letter.

For some reason, seeing the reunion you and Autumn had, made me think about a reunion I had with one of my college buddies.

A few years back, I ran into another college buddy that gave me Biggie's phone number. I hadn't seen him since our old A-state days and just knew it would be a fun time when we got to talking again. He was the kind of person that could get along with anyone. Of course, I view myself as that same kind of person. Another reason I knew we would share some laughs when I called him was because he always loved to laugh and crack jokes. As you know, I am somewhat conservative. But, Biggie is one of those people that will bring out the "crazy" in anyone.

When I called and he picked up the phone, I knew immediately it wasn't going to be the type of reunion I thought it would be. When he answered with "Hello!" I said "What's up, Biggie? You know who you're talkin' to?" He said "It's been some years, Tee, but you know cain't nobody forget that voice." The way he was talking let me know something was wrong. Being me and being the blunt kind of person that gets straight to the point, I asked what was going on because he just wasn't being himself.

What was happening was he was in mourning. A couple of weeks earlier, his sister and her husband had come off of a weekend trip and found their seventeen year old daughter dead on the floor of their home. It was obvious that she had been murdered.

In the conversation, he told me that the police had found the person that killed his niece and the guy had a made a confession.

When I asked him what was behind all of it, the story started to get really strange. Well, I remember thinking then that it was strange. Now, it's not so strange. At that time, what led to the murder was somewhat new to the regular world. Now, everyone and their mom has internet access.

He said his niece met a guy online. These stories came from the man's confession and from some of the murdered young lady's friends. The story was that he had posed as a high school student from across town. They lived in one of the largest cities in the country. Living in small town Arkansas, I guess that is possible. It definitely wouldn't have be en possible where I grew up.

In actuality, the guy was twenty-seven years old and they had been seeing each other for close to a year. When she would tell her parents she was going with some friends, a lot of the times she would be going to be with him.

On the weekend of the murder, she invited him over so they could spend some alone time since she would have the house to herself.

Before I continue I must tell you that a few days before the weekend hookup, she informed him that she was pregnant. No, she hadn't told her parents. Well, to make a long story short, he came over that weekend prepared to take her life.

It came out that he was married with two children. I guess he got scared of his wife finding out about the ongoing affair and the child Biggie's niece was carrying.

I'm not going to condemn the young lady for the choices she made. She was a kid. She wasn't yet knowledgeable in the ways and dangers the world outside of mom and dad. She thought she had found a boyfriend of her own age that she could spend fun times with during her high school years.

This letter isn't about the mistakes of a young lady. It's about the dangers of the internet.

Don't get me wrong. I'm not saying the internet is all bad. It, just like anything else, can offer some good and bad.

Back when that incident took place, law enforcement didn't know enough about internet predators to issue warnings like they do today.

Believe me when I say that a lot of people on the internet looking to meet someone, aren't who they say they are. You can think you're chatting with a nice young man and it can turn out to be a seventy-five year old man who just got out of prison for the rape and murder of a mother and her two daughters.

Another thing you need to consider regarding the internet is how you conduct your everyday life. Everyone has a cell phone with a camera on it these days. If you are caught doing something wrong or immoral, it can end up on Youtube or some other site. Whether you believe it or not, something like that can and probably will haunt you for the rest of your life. (of course, depending on what's put on there)

Bottom line is this. To be safe, use the internet for the boundless bits of information it offers to you as a student.

In chatting, unless you are chatting with a friend or associate that you know without a doubt means you no harm, don't chat. Above all, don't put anything remotely personal over the internet air. Although you think you have deleted it, it is always out there somewhere.

Also, there are people out there with the mentality of a great white shark. A great white swims (surfs) the waters (internet) all day with one purpose in mind. He wants to find palatable (gullible) prey (youngsters) to eat (take advantage of).

Be careful! And like I always tell you, if it's something you can't do in front of or show to Dad, Mom or whoever your legal-guardian is, it doesn't mean you any good.

Please let that one saturate you cranial capacity.

I love you,
TC

"Don't Be Scurred"

Ecclesiastes 9:11
" . . . but time and chance happen to them all."

Layla,

To me, one of the funniest, craziest characters created in a sitcom is the character "Hustle Man," played by Tracy Morgan on Martin Lawrence's show aptly named, "Martin."

Being as conservative as I am, back when Martin was in prime-time, I thought some of it was a little over the top. But, as I age, I am beginning to enjoy a good laugh more than ever before. For some reason, some of the shows that didn't particularly tickle my funny-bone back then, have me rolling now.

Getting back to Hustle-man: what I found so funny about him was how he looked for any opportunity to make a fast dollar. Whether it was selling pigeon on a stick during a snowstorm or if he was trying to get a recording deal by playing a saxophone with a kazoo for a mouthpiece, to me, Hustle man was hilarious.

He was what you would call a "street entrepreneur." And in reality, there isn't much difference in the street variety and their corporate counterparts. Of course, the main difference is money. (or in the case of the man on the street, the lack of money) Another difference is education. (or, again, in the case of the man on the street, the lack of an education)

Now, don't think I'm saying none of the people on the streets have a formal education. Some do have that "sheep-skin," but just haven't caught that lucky break yet. Being real, though, a great deal of the guys you see peddling stuff on the streets haven't graduated or even been to a school of higher learning.

So, why do I say there isn't much difference? Take a look at them both. For one, they both have that salesman mentality. Don't take "No" for an answer. As a matter of fact, most of them are so persistent they can get on your nerves sometimes. Secondly, they both realize that they are playing on numbers. Not everyone is going to buy their product and they know this. They also know the more people they approach, the more likely they are to getting a sale or whatever it is they are trying to push.

Yea, you know I would eventually get to it, so, here it comes. What is the relevance of the first page? It's this. "Don't be afraid to take chances."

Before I get into that, let me say that I don't mean take chances on something that doesn't make sense or something that will harm you or someone else.

Situation:

You are attending a school play with the young lady you consider your BFFL, (best friend for life). (I really don't know if that's proper texting prose, but for right now just go with it)

The play consists of the first act, an intermission and the second act.

During intermission, you and your "girl" step out to the ladies' room to stretch your legs and to see who else fell asleep during the first act.

When a member of the faculty comes into the restroom and announces that the second act is about to start, everyone else leaves. You try to leave, but sista-girl pulls you back and tells you to stay for a minute. At the same moment, you notice another girl who had just walked out, come back in. Now, this a girl you know, of course. But, you also know she is bad news. Not the kind of person you would want to be associated with.

It really surprises you when she goes to your friend and greets her like they have known each other for years. You're thinking, "What is going on?"

What's going on is, as you know, the bad seed is the female equivalent of the "dopeman" and she is about to make a transaction with your friend who expects you to join in on the festivities and get "blowed."

Probably one of the most successful and recognizable advertising slogans of all time came from the mind of

Nike. (Yea, the shoe company) They had a slogan that said "Just do it!"

From me, someone who loves you and wants you to become a success, when someone approaches you wanting you to buy some drugs or to partake in some casual relaxation methods that involve drug usage, remember to do just the opposite of what the Nike slogan said. "Just don't do it!"

And before you say, "What if it's just weed?" Don't! Marijuana is a drug. Plain and simple! No explanation needed.

I know without a doubt, there will be proponents of the legalization of marijuana that will argue that point. Oh well, it's still a drug. Whether you make it legal or not.

That is the part where I say don't be stupid when I say "Don't be afraid to take chances." Now, notice I didn't say, "Don't be afraid to take risks." The difference is, if you look up the word risk, you will see that it mentions the danger aspect of stepping out on a limb.

The option that presented itself to the young lady in the "Situation" above is definitely a risk rather than a chance.

I would describe a chance as any positive endeavor you conceive mentally and have the opportunity to act upon physically. It could be something as simple as you wanting to run for student council, or it could be something as complex as a new invention you dreamed up. If you have come up with something you want to make a run at, how will you succeed at it if you don't give it a try? Whatever it is, make sure you do your homework regarding the situation. No, that doesn't mean more actual homework. It means do your investigation and research on the topic. The more knowledgeable you are about anything, the more likely you are to succeed at it.

Just like it has been embedded in the brain of the street entrepreneur and his corporate counterpart, the more positive endeavors you make a run at, the more opportunities you give yourself to succeed.

Okay, you may understand it better if I said it like this, "Don't be scurred!"

I love you,
TC

Persevere, My Dear

James 1:12
"Blessed is the man who remains steadfast . . .
he will receive the crown . . ."

Hija,

Today, you accomplished something you have failed at the last two attempts you made at it. Actually, you achieved it the last part of the school year, last year. Today, it finally came into fruition with the start of practice and camp coming up. Of course, I'm referring to you making the senior high cheerleader squad. Now don't think I don't want you to be a cheerleader. You *know* without a doubt, that you always have had, have and always will have my full support in any positive endeavor you partake of. Let me just say I am more proud of you for knowing what you wanted to do and the determination you displayed in going after it. You wanted to be a cheerleader and you went after it and became one. The great thing about it is that you failed to make the squad twice on the middle school level. Then, you succeeded on the senior high level. Needless to say, that level is more competitive and one would think that it is a harder squad to make. That one little quality, perseverance, combined with hard work in school and respect for yourself and others will get you farther at this point in your life than anything.

We have talked about how I consider myself a late bloomer. Take this book for example. I can't tell you how many times in the past that I have started on different books, only to do a few chapters and allow something or someone to take my incentive. In all honesty, if I had finished all the books I have started, at least a couple of them would have been published.

Here's a quick little exercise for you. Take a minute and think of a time you tried to do something positive. Was there an obstacle that presented itself? I would bet a dollar to a dime that there was one. Every time you, me or anyone tries to do something to the good, something or someone offers a stumbling block. As your grandmother used to tell your uncles and me, "That ain't nothin' but the devil trying to stop you from doin' what God put you here to do."

Well, with this book, he has thrown monkey wrenches at me on a daily basis. Truth be told, he won a couple of the battles. The fact that you and others have the opportunity to read this book after it was published, shows that just like any other time, God won the war. God gave me motivation this time that I couldn't deny. Motivation that let me know eventually, this book had to be and would be finished. That motivation, if you don't know already, was and is you. I am extraordinarily proud of you, Cube!

I love you,
Daddy

P.S.

Now, you know, this is just like anything else.

If, for any reason, those grades drop below the honor-roll, cheering will take a hiatus.